Three States of Water

Water is everywhere! Our bodies are mostly water. So is our planet. Water can be a liquid, a solid, or a gas.

Drinking water is a liquid. Snow and ice are solids. Water vapor is a gas. When it cools, it forms steam.

Draw a rectangle around each form of water you see in these pictures. Then, find at least **10** differences between the scenes.

TALK ABOUT IT!

- How is snow different from liquid water?
- Where have you seen ice? What does ice feel like?

Properties of Matter

What words could you use to describe this can? You could say it is a hard, silver cylinder. You could say it is bumpy and stiff. These words tell about the can's properties. A **property** is one quality that an object possesses.

Some Properties of Matter	Examples
Color: What is the object's color?	blue, red, orange, purple, silver
Shape: What shape is the object?	cone, cylinder, cube, sphere
Texture: How does the object feel?	bumpy, rough, smooth
Hardness: How hard is the object?	hard, soft
Flexibility: How bendable is the object?	flexible, stiff

Write words from the chart to name some properties of each object below. Then find an object at home that shares a property with each object in the table. Write it in the table below. We did the first one to get you started.

Object	Properties	Object that shares a property
	yellow, smooth, flexible	A banana is yellow, too.

TALK ABOUT IT!

- Tell a friend or family member about the properties of each object.
- Name objects in your home that are soft. Name objects that are hard. Are any objects in your home flexible?

SECOND GRADE

2

AGES 7–8

Hands-On STEAM
Learning Fun Workbook

For information about permission to reproduce selections from this book for
an entire school or school district, please contact permissions@highlights.com.

Published by Highlights Learning • 815 Church Street • Honesdale, Pennsylvania 18431
ISBN: 978-1-64472-297-8
Mfg. 11/2020
Printed in Madison, WI, USA
First edition
10 9 8 7 6 5 4 3 2 1

For assistance in the preparation of this book, the editors would like to thank:
Vanessa Maldonado, MSEd; MS Literacy Ed. K–12; Reading/LA Consultant Cert.; K–5 Literacy Instructional Coach
Kristin Ward, MS Curriculum, Instruction, and Assessment; K–5 Mathematics Instructional Coach
Jump Start Press, Inc.

Solids and Liquids

What happens when you pour a drink from a bottle into a cup?

Matter that keeps its shape is **solid**. Matter that takes the shape of its container is **liquid**.

The bottle and the cup are solids. The juice is a liquid. The juice flows from the bottle into the cup. It takes the shape of its container.

> Matter is anything that takes up space.

Look at each picture. Write the word **solid** or **liquid** to complete each sentence.

	Coffee is a _____ The mug is a _____
	The bowl is a _____ A cracker is a _____ The soup is a _____
	The pool is a _____ The water is a _____ The hose is a _____

TALK ABOUT IT!
- What other liquids have you seen?
- What is another solid object that can hold a liquid?
- Why would liquids and solids need different tools for measuring?

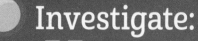

Investigate:
Household Objects

Choose 2 different objects from your home.

Complete the chart below. Draw a picture of one object at the top of each column. Write words to tell about each object's properties.

Properties	Object #1	Object #2
Color		
Shape		
Texture		
Hardness		
Flexibility		

TALK ABOUT IT!

- What objects did you choose? What properties of the objects are different? Are any of the objects' properties the same?
- What other objects in your home have some of the same properties?

Best Material for the Job

Would you want to use a pillow full of hard and bumpy rocks? Why not? Most people want a pillow that is comfortable to sleep on. People use materials that fit the **purpose**, or use, of an object.

Look at the objects below. Write the name of the object that best matches each clue.

sofa

hose

desk

baseball bat

You might sit on this **soft, firm** object to read a book. _____

People use this **hard** object to hit a ball. _____

People use this **flexible** object to move water. _____

A computer might sit on this **smooth** surface. _____

TALK ABOUT IT!

- Think about the properties of objects in your home. Why do you think mirrors are hard, smooth, and shiny?
- What words tell about the properties of your refrigerator? How do these properties fit its purpose?

Investigate:
Bridge the Gap!

🔍 **Can you build a bridge that will hold a hardcover book?**

1. Look at these bridges. Choose one as your model.

| arch bridge | beam bridge | suspension bridge | truss bridge |

2. Look around your home. What materials could you use to build your bridge?

_____

_____

3. Make a plan to build your bridge. Draw a picture of it. Show the materials you will use.

4. Gather all the materials. Follow your plan to build your bridge.

5. Test your bridge. Can it hold a hardcover book? What else can it hold?

TALK ABOUT IT!
- How did you decide what bridge to build?
- What could you do to make the bridge stronger? Try your ideas.

Which Materials to Use?

Luke loves to go camping with his family. They use different materials for different needs.

Read the purpose in each row. Circle the material that would be better for the purpose. Then find another material at your home that would fit each purpose. Draw it in the chart.

Purpose	Material		Another Object
Carrying water			
Making a fire			
Keeping things dry			
Making a comfortable place to sleep			

TALK ABOUT IT!

• Tell about the material you chose for each purpose. Why is it better?

• Now talk about what materials would be best for a tent. A tent should be big enough to hold people inside. It should be sturdy enough to stop rain from getting in.

Investigate:
Sturdy Materials

Look at this giant redwood tree. It is one of the tallest types of trees in the world and is naturally very strong.

🔍 **What materials work best to make a tall, sturdy structure?**

> **YOU NEED:**
>
> • materials for the base of your structure: cardboard, paper plates, or box lids • materials to make the structure taller: craft sticks, cardboard tubes, straws, or cups • materials to connect different parts: tape, clay, or glue • yardstick

1. Start with the base. Add materials to build a tall structure. Use a yardstick to measure the height of your creation.

2. Use your hands to shake the surface under or near your creation. What happens to your structure?

3. Add materials or change the design of your structure to make it sturdier. Try to keep the height the same or make it taller.

4. Test your new creation. Shake the surface again and see what happens.

5. Continue testing new ideas. Combine ideas until you have the sturdiest structure you can make.

TALK ABOUT IT!

• What materials were the strongest? Describe their properties.

• Did any materials make the structure taller but weaker?

From Smaller Pieces

People make many objects by putting smaller pieces together. Take a close look at these objects. What smaller pieces make up each one?

The pieces of an object may be different materials. For example, the bicycle has metal, rubber, and leather pieces.

Draw a line to match each tower with the set of blocks used to make it.

TALK ABOUT IT!

- Count the blocks in each tower. Which tower has the most blocks? Which tower has the fewest blocks?

- Look around your home. What objects do you see that are made from smaller pieces?

 Invent:
From the Same Pieces

What have you made from toy blocks or building bricks? These toys are fun to play with. You can build, tear down, and build something new.

 What can you make with toy building materials?

YOU NEED:
- toy building blocks
- crayons or markers

1. Use the blocks to build any structure you can think up.

2. Draw a picture of your **Building 1** in the chart below.

3. Take apart the pieces in Building 1. Design and build another structure. Make sure you use all the same pieces again.

4. Draw a picture of your **Building 2** in the chart below.

Building 1	Building 2

TALK ABOUT IT!
- How are the buildings you made alike? How are they different?
- What other buildings or objects could you make from the same blocks?

Cook, Melt, Burn

What happens when you heat something? Three ways to add heat to matter are **cooking**, **melting**, and **burning**. Each process changes matter in different ways.

Read the description for each pair of pictures. Write **before** under the picture that shows matter before heating. Write **after** under the picture that shows how the matter changes with heat.

When matter **cooks**, some of its properties change. A pancake starts as gooey batter. When it is cooked, it gets firmer. The color gets darker.	 _____	 _____
When matter **melts**, it changes from a solid to a liquid. This ice pop melts in the hot sun.	 _____	 _____
When matter **burns**, it changes into different matter. Paper burns and turns into ash.	 _____	 _____

TALK ABOUT IT!

• Think of a food your family cooks. How does the food change when it is cooked?

• How is ash different from paper?

Adding Heat

Hot, hot, hot! In a pizza restaurant, heat is added to different materials. Write **cook**, **melt**, or **burn** to tell what each picture shows.

_____ _____ _____

Can you find the **13** objects in this Hidden Pictures puzzle?

flower

teacup

artist's brush

sailboat

wedge of orange

comb

fishhook

hammer

envelope

candle

pencil

golf club

football

TALK ABOUT IT!

- What does pizza dough look and feel like?
- How do the properties of pizza dough change when heat is added?
- What happens to pizza toppings when heat is added?

Cool It!

When matter freezes, it changes from a liquid to a solid.

What words could describe the surface of this lake?

The lake is _____.

Its surface is _____.

Heat was taken away from the water in the lake. The water on the surface froze into ice.

A berry smoothie is a liquid. Put an **X** on the picture that shows the smoothie in a liquid state. Circle the picture that shows the smoothie after it has been frozen.

There are **6** words (not pictures!) hidden in the zoo. Can you find ARCTIC, FISH, HABITAT, ICE, SWIM, and TUXEDO?

TALK ABOUT IT!
- Why are people able to skate on ice but not on water?
- What do people do to make ice pops?
- Which parts of the zoo scene show something frozen?

Investigate:
Solid to Liquid and Back

How can you change matter from a solid to a liquid? Can the matter change back to a solid?

 Melting Ice Cream

YOU NEED:
- ice cream, sherbet, frozen yogurt, or a frozen ice pop • a bowl

1. With a parent's permission, put a scoop of ice cream or an ice pop in a bowl.
2. Place the bowl in a sunny place.
3. Wait for the ice cream to melt.
4. Put the bowl of melted ice cream in the freezer. Wait at least 1 hour. Check on the ice cream. What happened?

🔍 Make a Tasty Treat: Chocolate Banana Pops

YOU NEED:
- 4 bananas • butter knife • cookie sheet, lined with wax paper
- wooden craft sticks • 1 cup semi-sweet chocolate chips
- toppings, such as granola, candy, nuts, or sprinkles

1. Peel 4 bananas and cut them in half (across). Place them on the cookie sheet lined with wax paper.
2. Put a craft stick into each piece of banana. Place the tray of bananas in the freezer for about an hour.
3. While the bananas are freezing, ask an adult to melt 1 cup of chocolate chips in the microwave.
4. Take out the bananas. Dip them into the melted chocolate. Cover them with toppings, as desired.
5. Put the bananas back on the cookie sheet and freeze them for 3 to 5 hours. What happened to the chocolate? Eat and enjoy!

What Plants Need

What do plants need to live and grow? Plants need **sunlight** and **water**. They also need **air**, **nutrients**, and **space to grow**.

A greenhouse is a special place where people grow plants.

Outdoor plants get water from rain. People can also help plants get water. Plants get nutrients from soil.

TALK ABOUT IT!

Answer these questions about the greenhouse:

• Describe the walls and the roof. Why do you think they were built this way?

• What can people buy here to help them water plants?

• What can people buy here to help plants get nutrients?

• How might growing plants in a greenhouse be different from growing them outside?

Growing Plants

Look at these plants! Only one plant has what it needs to live and grow. Circle that plant. Tell how it looks different from the other two plants.

Which blossom grew from which pot? Follow the tangled vines to find the answer.

TALK ABOUT IT!

- Do you think the plants in this maze are having their needs met? Why or why not?

- Have you ever helped a plant grow? What did you do?

Investigate:
Plants and Water

A drought occurs when there is little rainfall for a long period of time. The land becomes dry. Plants may struggle to stay alive.

🔍 What happens when a plant does not get the water it needs?

YOU NEED:

- grass seeds and soil
- 2 pots or small plastic containers
- tape • crayons or markers

In this investigation, you will plant grass seeds in 2 pots. Both pots get sunlight. But only 1 pot gets water.

MAKE PREDICTIONS

Predict what will happen. Which seeds will grow better? Draw pictures to show your predictions.

Predictions	
Seeds with Water	Seeds with No Water

TALK ABOUT IT!

- Tell about your predictions. What do your drawings show?
- How might the seeds grow differently? Why?

DO THE INVESTIGATION

1. Put soil in each pot. Plant a handful of grass seeds in each. Use about the same number of seeds in each pot.

2. Put a piece of tape on each pot. Label one pot "Water" and the other pot "No Water." Then place both pots in a sunny place.

3. Over the next 2 weeks, water the seeds in the "Water" pot. (NOTE: Be sure not to use too much water. The soil should be moist, but not soaking.) DO NOT water the seeds in the "No Water" pot. Watch how the seeds grow.

4. After 2 weeks, observe the results. Draw your observations in the first row of the **Results** chart below.

5. Repeat step 4. Then draw in the second row of the **Results** chart below to show how each pot of seeds looks after about a month's time.

DISCUSS THE RESULTS

Compare the results to your predictions on page 18.

Time	Results	
	Seeds with Water	Seeds with No Water
after 2 weeks		
after 1 month		

Investigate:
Plants Depend on Animals

Look closely at the bee. The little yellow specks all over its body are pollen grains. Plants create pollen to help them make more plants. Animals such as bees move pollen from plant to plant. This helps the plant grow seeds or fruit.

Butterflies and some birds eat nectar from flowers. When an animal stops to eat nectar, pollen may stick to its body.

🔍 Show Pollination

YOU NEED:

• **sheet of dark paper** • **crayons or markers** • **cotton ball** • **small dish of flour**

1. Draw a flower on a dark sheet of paper.

2. Dip the cotton ball in flour.

3. Shake it over the flower drawing to distribute "pollen."

4. Tell how this would help the flower if it was pollen.

Help the animals go from START to FINISH to spread pollen from plant to plant. Which one visits the most flowers along the way?

START

START

START

FINISH

FINISH

FINISH

Flower Flies

Read the article below. Then answer the questions.

This Fly Is in Disguise

By Alison Pearce Stevens, PhD

You stand in a garden. A quiet hum reaches your ears. You see a small insect hovering near your head. You turn to look, and it darts out of sight. There it is again! You move slowly. You can see yellow and black stripes on it.

Is it a bee? A wasp? It lands on a flower, and you take a closer look.

Bees and wasps fold their wings onto their backs when they stop flying. But this insect's wings stick out like a fly's. That's because it *is* a fly! A flower fly.

Many flower flies look like bees and wasps. This helps keep them safe from animals that may want to eat them. Insects with yellow and black stripes usually have stingers. Insect eaters, such as some birds, small mammals, frogs, and toads, need to get stung only once to know that stripes mean trouble. Flower flies can't sting. But insect eaters see the stripes and leave the flies alone.

Flower flies spend most of their time looking for food. Like bees, flower flies eat pollen and nectar. This makes them easy to find in a garden full of blooming flowers.

Flower flies are helpful garden insects. Adult flower flies move pollen from one flower to another, which helps some flowers grow into fruit. The young flower-fly larvae help by eating tiny insects called aphids. Aphids suck the juice out of plants, which can hurt the plants.

WRITE ABOUT IT!

1. How are flower flies like bees and wasps? How are they different?

_____

_____

2. In what ways do flower flies and flower-fly larvae help plants?

_____

_____

Animals Move Seeds

In what ways can animals help plants spread their seeds?

Read each description on the left. Draw a line to the picture that best matches the description.

An animal may carry seeds in its mouth. It may drop the seeds in a new location.

○   ○

Some plants have seeds covered in burrs. The burrs have hooks, which can cling to an animal's fur. The animal moves around. The burrs fall off.

○   ○

Some animals bury seeds to eat later. They may not retrieve all the seeds. The seeds may grow into new plants.

○   ○

TALK ABOUT IT!

• Have you ever seen an animal eating or burying seeds? Describe what you saw.

• Look at the animal with burrs in its fur. Why do you think its fur picks up burrs easily?

 Invent:

A Seed Mover

Think about how animals move seeds in different ways.

 What can you make to pick up and move seeds?

YOU NEED:

Assorted materials, depending on the design of your model:

- To pick up seeds, you might use wooden spoons, tweezers, or pieces of cardboard.
- To make seeds stick, you might use pieces of tape, hook-and-loop fasteners, or clay.
- seeds, acorns, or burrs • drawing materials

1. Draw a picture to plan your design.

2. Use materials to build your seed-moving tool.

3. Test your tool. Try picking up the seeds and moving them to a new location.

My Design

EVALUATE AND REDESIGN

- How well did your tool work? Were you able to pick up any seeds? Could you carry them to a new location?

- Did you have any problems with your design? How might you fix them?

- Try out different designs and materials and compare the results.

TALK ABOUT IT!

- What materials worked best to pick up and move seeds?
- Compare your tool to one of the animals on page 22.

Rain Forests

A **rain forest** is one type of habitat. Rain forests are the wettest places on Earth. They are also home to more than half of the plants, animals, and insects found on Earth.

Read the chart below to learn more about a rain forest.

A habitat is a place where plants and animals live to meet their needs.

What Can You Find in the Layers of a Rain Forest?			
Emergent Layer the tops of the trees	**Canopy** treetops that grow close together	**Understory** dark area with low trees, bushes, and ferns	**Forest Floor** the ground; very little sunlight reaches here
• Generally smaller animals, such as eagles, hummingbirds, sloths, and spider monkeys, because treetops can't support heavy weight	• Many types of birds, such as toucans, macaws, and cockatoos • Mammals that like to climb and move from tree to tree, such as monkeys, orangutans, sloths, lemurs, and squirrels • Insects • Snakes and lizards • Tree frogs	• Animals and insects that live on and in tree bark, such as beetles, spiders, frogs, snakes, lizards, and mammals like the kinkajou and the leopard • Birds, such as hummingbirds, that eat nectar from plants	• Larger mammals, such as gorillas, civets, tapirs, anteaters, leopards, jaguars, wild boar, and deer • Many insects • Spiders, such as tarantulas • Snakes

Which 2 toucan pictures are exactly alike?

Deserts

Deserts are the driest places on Earth. They get very little rain. Plants and animals that live in deserts have features that help them adapt to their dry habitat.

Look at this desert tortoise. It spends most of its time in burrows of rock or soil. Its body functions slow down to deal with extreme hot or cold temperatures and lack of water. When a desert tortoise comes out of its burrow, it eats wildflowers. The "juicy" plants give it water as well as food.

Circle each animal and plant that you think lives in a desert.

TALK ABOUT IT!

- What type of plants live in a desert? How do you think they store water?
- Look at the animals and plants you did not circle. Why would it be hard for them to live in a desert?

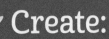
Create:
A Shoebox Habitat

Make your own rain forest or desert in a shoebox.

> **YOU NEED:**
> - shoebox • construction paper
> - crayons, markers, or colored pencils
> - glue • scissors • colored clay or play dough

Mawsynram, a rain-forest village in India, is the wettest place on Earth. It gets about 460 inches of rain each year. The Atacama Desert in Chile is the driest place. It gets less than 1 inch of rain each year.

1. Choose a habitat: rain forest or desert. Look online for pictures of your habitat. Find out what plants and animals live there.

2. Put the shoebox on its side. Draw and color a background for the habitat. Glue it to the back of the shoebox.

3. Draw and cut out plants that live in the habitat. Glue them so they stand up in the shoebox.

4. Use clay or play dough to make animals for the habitat. Put them in the box.

5. Write a guide to your habitat. Tell about the plants and animals that live there.

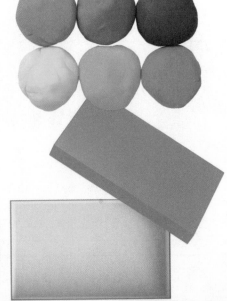

Investigate:
Your Habitat

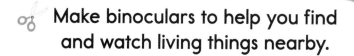

What plants and animals live in the habitat where you are?

✂ **Make binoculars to help you find and watch living things nearby.**

YOU NEED:
• paper-towel tube • tempera paints • cork • colored masking tape • tacky glue

1. Cut the paper-towel tube in half. Paint the tubes. (You could also paint the cork.) Allow the paint to dry completely.

2. Add colored masking tape to the top and bottom of each tube.

3. Use tacky glue to attach the side of the cork to one tube. Hold the cork in place for a few seconds to allow the glue to set.

4. Glue the other cardboard tube to the cork. Hold it in place for a few seconds. Set the binoculars aside and allow the glue to dry completely.

5. Use your binoculars to look for plants and animals around the place where you live.

6. Draw to show some living things you see.

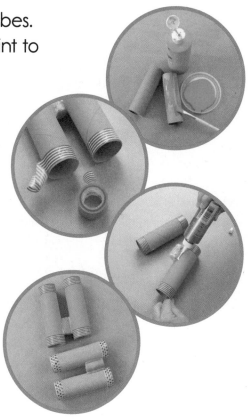

TALK ABOUT IT!

Tell about the area around your home. What is the weather like throughout the year? Are there forests nearby, or a desert, or an ocean? What living things are able to meet their needs in the area?

Slow Changes

Some changes on Earth happen so slowly, it takes many years to see their effects.

How do slow changes affect Earth?

Look at the Grand Canyon. Over millions of years, the Colorado River pushed away parts of the earth. These slow changes revealed layers of beautiful rock. And the changes formed the long, deep valleys of the Grand Canyon.

It's time for a ride through the Grand Canyon. Can you find and circle the 11 objects in this Hidden Pictures puzzle?

bow

boat

fan

toothbrush

flashlight

strawberry

shoe

arrow

ice-cream cone

fish

rabbit

TALK ABOUT IT!

• Why do you think it took millions of years for the Grand Canyon to form?

• What other changes on Earth happen slowly?

Slow Changes, Fast Changes

Imagine you are sitting in your home. All of a sudden, the ground below you shakes. The walls vibrate. Objects around you fall over. This is what it's like to experience an earthquake.

Do you think an earthquake changes Earth quickly or slowly?

Each of the events below changes Earth. Circle the correct word to tell if it changes Earth quickly or slowly.

An earthquake changes Earth

quickly   slowly

A hurricane changes water and land

quickly   slowly

Water changes rocks and forms a canyon

quickly   slowly

TALK ABOUT IT!

• Have you ever seen extreme weather, such as hurricane-force wind? How did it change the land and water around you?

• Which do you think are more powerful: changes that occur quickly or those that occur slowly? Why?

Volcanoes

A **volcano** is a hole in the Earth's surface that melted rock breaks through. Liquid rock called **magma** rises toward a volcano's vent. When a volcano erupts, ash and gas burst into the air. When magma reaches the surface, it's called **lava**. Lava flows down the sides of the volcano. This event causes changes that occur quickly.

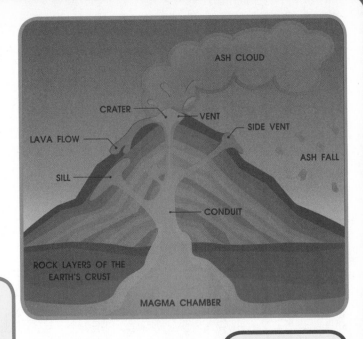

TALK ABOUT IT!

What questions do you have about volcanoes? Where could you look to find answers to your questions?

The fun is about to erupt! There are **19** words related to volcanoes hidden in the grid. Look for them up, down, across, backward, and diagonally. We found one to get you started.

ACTIVE
ASH
BASALT
BLAST
CINDER CONE
CRATER
DORMANT
ERUPT
FISSURE
HOT SPOT
LANDSLIDE
LAVA
MAGMA
MOLTEN ROCK
MOUNTAIN
PUMICE
SPATTER
TREMOR
VENT

Investigate:
A Volcano Erupting

🔍 What happens when a volcano erupts?
How can an eruption cause fast changes?

YOU NEED:

- a small jar (such as a baby food jar) for the inside of the volcano
- materials to make the volcano cone: clay, cardboard, a dirt mound, etc.
- baking soda • liquid dish soap • red and yellow food coloring • vinegar

NOTE: This investigation may get messy, so consider working outside. If you work inside, cover a large, flat surface with newspapers or plastic before beginning.

1. Place the jar in the center of your working area.

2. Build up your volcano around the jar. You may use clay, decorated cardboard, or even dirt. You should cover the sides of the jar completely.

3. Add 2 tablespoons of baking soda to the jar.

4. Add 1 tablespoon of the liquid dish soap.

5. Add about 4 drops each of red and yellow food coloring.

6. Prepare for the eruption. Count down: 5, 4, 3, 2, 1. Then pour 2 tablespoons of vinegar into the mixture. Watch what happens next!

TALK ABOUT IT!

- What happened when you poured in the vinegar?
- How was the reaction like a volcano erupting?

Monument Valley

Water and wind are powerful forces of nature. They can cause both slow and quick changes on Earth.

Erosion occurs when parts of Earth's surface are slowly worn away. A body of water, such as a river, can push away bits of Earth and change the shape of the land. Wind can hit a rock formation and carry away pieces of it.

Read the passage about Monument Valley. Then answer the questions on the next page.

How Monument Valley Came to Be

The desert is an ever-changing place. Some 250 million years ago, giant sand dunes covered the southwestern United States.

To the east, wind and water eroded a great mountain chain. Bits of rock from these mountains swept westward. They added new layers of sand to the desert. In time, the land hardened into sandstone.

Millions of years passed. Waters washed across the lands and retreated.

Erosion again shaped the land. In spots, the sandstone was protected by flat caps of harder rock. The sandstone underneath each cap remained. But wind and water swept away the rest, carving fantastic forms out of the red sandstone. Today these forms make up the best-known landscape in the West—the spires, buttes, and mesas of Monument Valley.

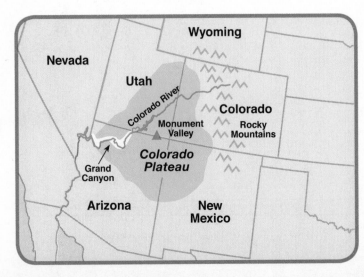

1. What words in the passage show that Monument Valley formed slowly?

_____

_____

2. Explain how both wind and water helped form Monument Valley.

_____

_____

3. What type of rock makes up the formations in Monument Valley? What protected the forms from being swept away by wind or water?

_____

_____

Many people think the formations in Monument Valley look like animals or objects. The monuments below are named for a camel, an elephant, and a mitten. What do you think each of these formations looks like?

The Effects of Erosion

Welcome to the town of Dinosaur, Colorado! It is home to Dinosaur National Monument, a park shared by Colorado and Utah. Over many years, erosion moved rock pieces there, revealing dinosaur remnants and rock carvings.

These visitors want to explore the park's rugged canyons. Help them follow the path from START to FINISH. Letters along the correct path will spell something the visitors hope to see. Write the letters in order here:

____ ____ ____ ____ ____ ____

TALK ABOUT IT!

- What do the visitors hope to see? Why might they want to see them?
- Look at the photos on pages 28 and 32 and the maze above. How are the Grand Canyon, Monument Valley, and Dinosaur National Monument alike? What do all three places show about erosion?

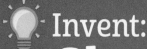 # Invent:
Slowing Down Erosion

People use different objects and structures to try to slow down erosion.

People planted these trees as a **windbreak**. The trees slow down wind erosion from affecting grass and crops.

People built this **seawall** to slow down water and wind erosion of the beach.

 What can you make to help slow down wind or water erosion?

YOU NEED:

- flat tray, shallow cardboard box, or shallow plastic box
- sand or dirt • water • a straw • materials to build your structure: toy blocks, toy houses or trees, shells, craft sticks, cardboard, etc.

1. In the tray or box, create a model of land that is at risk of erosion. You might use sand to make a beach or dirt to make land on either side of a river.

2. Add a small amount of water to see how water erosion might affect the land. Use the straw to blow air on the sand or dirt. See how wind erosion might affect the land.

3. Draw a picture to design the structure you will build to help slow down erosion.

4. Choose materials and build your structure. Add it to your model.

5. Use water and the straw to test water and wind erosion again. See how well your structure works.

EVALUATE AND REDESIGN

- Did you have any problems with your design? How might you fix them?
- Try out different designs and materials and compare the results.

Maps

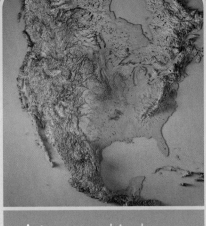

Have you ever used a map? A map is a drawing of a place. It shows features of the place, such as roads and waterways. It also shows how far it is from one location to another. A map is a helpful tool people can use to find their way around.

Can you find the correct city on each map? Use the compass rose to help you. Write each city's name on the line below each map.

A topographical map is a special kind of map. It shows the shapes of land, including mountains and valleys, and bodies of water.

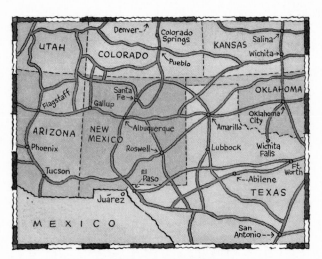

1. South of Pueblo
   West of Amarillo
   East of Tucson
   North of Gallup

_____

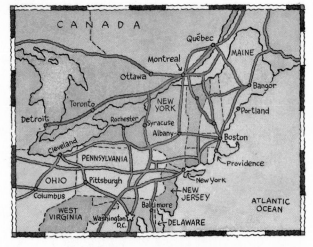

2. South of Ottawa
   West of Syracuse
   East of Cleveland
   North of Rochester

_____

TALK ABOUT IT!
What states are shown on each map? What countries?

 # Create:
A Tape Town Map

YOU NEED:
- several pieces of cardstock • colorful tape
- markers • toy cars and people

1. Choose a piece of cardstock. Use tape to create roads and paths for a certain part of the town, city, or neighborhood where you live.

2. Draw any parks, lakes, and other important features.

3. Repeat steps 1 and 2 for other parts of your town.

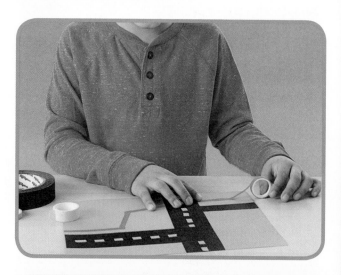

4. Place the maps together to show how the parts of your town connect.

5. Add toy cars, people, and buildings. Explore your town!

TALK ABOUT IT!
- Tell about your town. What roads do you take to get to school?
- What is your favorite place to go in your town? Why?

Bodies of Water

This picture shows what Earth looks like from space. All of the blue space you see is water. More than 70 percent of Earth's surface is water. That means there is more water than land on our planet.

Read the information in the chart to find out about different bodies of water.

Body of Water	Fresh/Salt Water?	Size
A **pond** is a small body of water. It is surrounded by land.	fresh water	smaller than a lake
A **lake** is deeper than a pond. Its water does not flow.	most are fresh water	larger than a pond
A **river** flows into another body of water. It has land on two sides.	most are fresh water	smaller than an ocean
An **ocean** is a large body of water. Oceans make up most of the water on Earth.	salt water	largest bodies of water

Use the information in the chart to help you identify the body of water in each photo below. Use the word box to help.

WORD BOX

pond   lake   river   ocean

_____ _____ _____ _____

TALK ABOUT IT!
- How can you tell which body of water each picture shows?
- What bodies of water have you seen? Describe each one.

On the Water

People can use boats and ships to travel across the ocean. Some ships transport goods from one country to another.

Read each name of a boat or ship. Point to that type of vessel in each picture.

Which type of vessel in these pictures can carry the most people? Which type is the smallest?

cargo ship   cruise ship   rowboat   sailboat   yacht

Now circle the differences you see between these pictures.

TRY THIS!

Can you make a paper boat that floats? Try different types of paper and different boat styles. Test them in a sink or tub of water. Refine your design as needed.

Icy "Islands"

In ocean waters near each polar ice sheet, chunks of freshwater ice—as small as a bed or as big as a small country—float in the salty sea. They come from glaciers and other ice formations that formed on land 1,000 or more years ago. When pieces at the edge of these ice masses break off and fall into an ocean or lake, the big floating chunks are called **icebergs**.

Many icebergs look white. That's due to air bubbles that were trapped as snow fell and packed down on the glacier.

Beware of icy conditions ahead! Circle the **19** words containing ICE hidden in the grid. The word *ICE* has been replaced with 🧊. Look up, down, across, backward, and diagonally. We did one to get you started.

ADVICE		NOTICE
BICEPS		OVERPRICED
CHOICES		POLICE
DEVICE		PRACTICE
ICEBERG		SERVICE
ICEBOX		~~SPICE~~
ICEMAKER		TRICERATOPS
JUSTICE		TWICE
LICORICE		VOICEMAIL
NICEST		

```
O V E R P R 🧊 D S L Y O P
U 🧊 F I B C A S O I S W O
E R 🧊 P F O N O V C 🧊 U L
N 🧊 L D H R K O S O O V 🧊
N J D A V 🧊 E U T R H O V
🧊 O E Q C S T K 🧊 🧊 C 🧊 E
L T C E E E P 🧊 A S N M D
P A E R I A X 🧊 B M N A D
R R C H O A T T B E 🧊 🧊 I 🧊
A D V 🧊 T V W S E S R L O
C 🧊 J U S T 🧊 🧊 S P O G S
T F S E R V 🧊 N S 🧊 B O X
🧊 N S P O T A R 🧊 R T O W
```

TALK ABOUT IT!

Name one type of animal that may be found on a polar ice sheet.

Create:
An Ice Lantern

✂ Create a warm glow on a cold day!

YOU NEED:

- 2 plastic containers (1 small and 1 large)   • sturdy tape
- coins   • tap water   • waterproof, battery-operated candle
- sand and seashells (optional)   • food coloring (optional)

1. Find 2 plastic storage containers of different sizes. The small one should fit into the large one with an inch or more of space all around.

2. Use packing tape or duct tape to suspend the small container inside the large one. Place coins in the small container for a little weight.

3. Pour water into the large container (not the small one) until water is an inch from the top. If you'd like, add sand and seashells to the bottom of the large container, or add food coloring to the water.

4. Set the container in the freezer. Or if the temperature is below freezing, leave it outside.

5. When the water is frozen solid, remove the small container. If it doesn't lift out easily, ask an adult to pour warm water into the small container to loosen it.

6. Remove the outer container. If it's stuck, ask an adult to turn it upside down (supporting the ice so it won't fall and break) and hold it under warm running water until it loosens.

7. Set the ice lantern outdoors. Choose a surface that won't be damaged by water (or food coloring). Put a waterproof, battery-operated candle in the center. Watch it glow!

TALK ABOUT IT!

- How is your ice lantern like an iceberg?
- What else could you add to an ice lantern to make a different design?

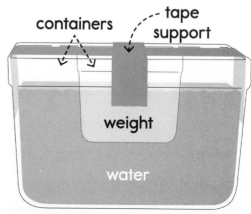

containers
tape support
weight
water

Engineering Solutions

Imagine you need to get an object that is on a shelf out of your reach. You have a problem. What will you do to solve it? Maybe you will find a stepstool to stand on. You will likely try out different solutions until you find one that works.

Engineers are scientists who analyze problems. They ask questions and design and build solutions.

The steps you follow to invent something are called the engineering design process.

Look at the object in each row. Name a problem it helps to solve.

	_____ _____ _____
	_____ _____ _____
	_____ _____ _____

TALK ABOUT IT!

• Find an object in your home. Can it be used to solve a problem?

• What is one problem you have? What could you design to solve it?

• Ask friends and family members what problems they would like to solve with new inventions.

Invent:

A Toy Solution

 **What can you make to help you organize and store small toy pieces?**

Do you play with toy building bricks that have small pieces? Or do you have any dolls, figures, or craft sets that have tiny accessories? Small toy pieces often get separated from larger pieces. They may be misplaced or lost. The vacuum cleaner may suck them up!

Design and build a system to help you keep small toy pieces safe and organized.

STEP 1: ASK QUESTIONS

- What can you use to help you keep small toy pieces together?
- How can you prevent small pieces from falling out of a container?
- What can you use to separate and organize pieces that are different types and different sizes?

STEP 2: DESIGN A SOLUTION

Draw a design of the solution you would like to make.

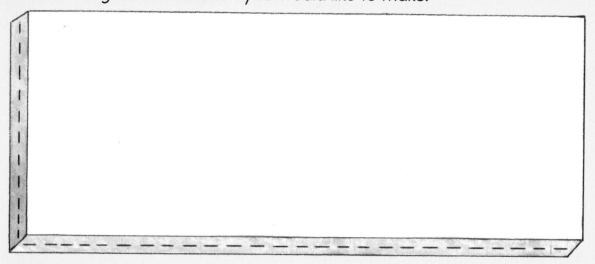

Turn the page for the next steps.

 Invent:

A Toy Solution

STEP 3: MAKE A MODEL
Follow your plan to make your solution.

YOU NEED:
- materials you might use to hold small toy pieces:
  plastic containers, an old shoebox, jars, etc.
- materials to keep the container closed: tape, rubber bands, clips, etc.
- materials to separate sections for organization:
  small pieces of cardboard, craft sticks, plastic bags, etc.

STEP 4: TEST THE MODEL
1. Put your small toy pieces into the organizing system you made.
2. Carry the box or container to a new location.
   Move it and shake it.
3. See how well the system holds small pieces
   and keeps them organized.

STEP 5: EVALUATE AND REDESIGN
- How well did your solution work? Did any
  small pieces fall out or get lost?
- What could you change to make the storage
  container sturdier or leak-proof?
- Try out different designs and materials
  and compare the results.

TALK ABOUT IT!
- Why do small toy pieces often sink down to the bottom of a toy box?
- What might happen when the vacuum cleaner "eats" a toy?

Highlights

Congratulations!

SECOND GRADE 2

_____
(your name)

worked hard
and finished the

Hands-On
STEAM

Learning Fun Workbook

Glossary

absorbency a property of matter that tells whether an object can soak up a liquid

burning adding heat to matter in a way that changes it into different matter

cooking adding heat to matter in a way that changes it irreversibly

desert a type of habitat that gets very little rain

drought occurs when there is little rainfall for a long period of time

earthquake a sudden shaking of the ground caused by movements in the Earth

engineers people who use science to solve problems

erosion occurs when part of Earth's surface wears away, often from water or wind

flexibility a property of matter that tells whether an object can bend

freezing taking heat away from matter to change it in a way that is reversible

habitat a place where plants and animals can live and meet their needs

hurricane a large storm with powerful winds

iceberg large chunks of freshwater ice floating in the waters around the north and south poles

lake a body of water larger than a pond and surrounded by land

lava liquid rock that has erupted from a volcano

liquid matter that takes the shape of its container

magma liquid rock inside a volcano

map a drawing of a place

matter anything that takes up space

melting adding heat to matter to change it from a solid to a liquid in a way that is reversible

nutrients minerals and other matter from the soil that plants need to live

ocean a very large body of salt water

pollen a powder that plants create to help them make more plants

pond a small body of water surrounded by land

rain forest a type of habitat that gets a lot of rain

river a body of water that flows into another body of water; has land on two sides

seawall a wall built to slow down water and wind erosion of a beach

solid matter that keeps its shape

texture a property of matter that tells how an object feels

volcano a hole in the Earth's surface that melted rock breaks through

windbreak a wall or row of objects that slows down wind erosion from affecting grass and crops

Answers

Page 3
Three States of Water

Page 14
Cool It!

Page 24
Rain Forests

Page 34
The Effects of Erosion
FOSSILS

Page 36
Maps

1. Santa Fe   2. Toronto

Page 10
From Smaller Pieces

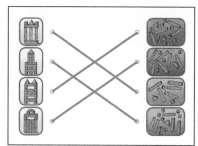

Page 17
Growing Plants

Flower A — Pot 3

Flower B — Pot 5

Flower C — Pot 4

Flower D — Pot 2

Flower E — Pot 1

Page 28
Slow Changes

Page 39
On The Water

Page 13
Adding Heat

Page 20
Plants Depend on Animals

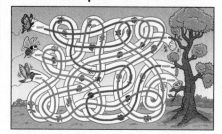

The bee visits the most flowers.

Page 30
Volcanoes

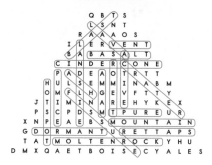

Page 40
Icy "Islands"

Extend the Learning

Want to explore further? Encourage your child's interest and curiosity in the topics throughout the book. Here are some ideas to get you started.

Properties of Matter *(pages 2–9)*

Solids and liquids are two forms of matter. Work with your child to explore ways to measure each form. Gather a variety of solids and liquids, such as small toys and art materials and small bottles of juice and cooking oil. Then use tools such as a kitchen scale, a measuring cup, and a tape measure to measure the solids and liquids. Discuss: *What are some measurements you found? Are some tools better for measuring solids or liquids? Why?*

Chemical Reactions *(pages 12–15)*

Adding or taking away heat can cause matter to change. Invite your child to observe these changes while helping to prepare dinner. As you prepare each food, talk about the changes that occur. Do you have to thaw frozen foods? Boil potatoes? Grill meat? Fry an egg? How does each food change when heat is added? Help your child identify which changes are reversible or irreversible.

Plants *(pages 16–19)*

Different plants need different amounts of water and sunlight. Have your child create a plant care guide for your houseplants or the plants in your yard. Help your child identify a few of your plants and do research online to find out how to care for each of them. He or she can create index cards with brief care instructions and place them in a convenient place for future reference.

Plants Depend on Animals *(pages 20–23)*

Many animals help move seeds from place to place. In the fall, go on a seed hunt in a local park with your child. Can you find holly berries, acorns, chestnuts, maple "wings," seed pods, and other seeds? When you return home, work with your child to find information and photos online for each kind of seed you found. Discuss: *How do certain animals help move some of the seeds you found? Why do you think they do that?*